DATA BOX

ENNA

T0111904

| Process: | | # of Operators |
| Verb/Noun: | | |

Operator Cycle Time: OCT	
Machine Cycle Time: MCT	
Value-Added Time: VAT	
Changeover Time: C/O	
Quality: % Defects/Scrap Rate	
Productivity: Units/Person/Hour	
Total Space: Sq. Feet/Meters	
Value-Added Space: (sq.ft/m)	
Product Travel: Feet/Meters	
Product Flow: Push/Pull	Push Pull
Information Flow: Manual/Electronic	Manual Elec.
Shifts: NET Avail. Time (Sec.)	Net Avail:
Inventory: INV Before:	After:

DATA BOX

ENNA

© Enna 2009
www.enna.com

Process:		# of Operators
Verb/Noun:		

Operator Cycle Time: OCT	
Machine Cycle Time: MCT	
Value-Added Time: VAT	
Changeover Time: C/O	
Quality: % Defects/Scrap Rate	
Productivity: Units/Person/Hour	
Total Space: Sq. Feet/Meters	
Value-Added Space: (sq.ft/m)	
Product Travel: Feet/Meters	
Product Flow: Push/Pull	Push Pull
Information Flow: Manual/Electronic	Manual Elec.
Shifts: NET Avail. Time (Sec.)	Net Avail:
Inventory: INV Before:	After:

DATA BOX

ENNA

© Enna 2009
www.enna.com

Process:		# of Operators
Verb/Noun:		

Operator Cycle Time: OCT	
Machine Cycle Time: MCT	
Value-Added Time: VAT	
Changeover Time: C/O	
Quality: % Defects/Scrap Rate	
Productivity: Units/Person/Hour	
Total Space: Sq. Feet/Meters	
Value-Added Space: (sq.ft/m)	
Product Travel: Feet/Meters	
Product Flow: Push/Pull	Push Pull
Information Flow: Manual/Electronic	Manual Elec.
Shifts: NET Avail. Time (Sec.)	Net Avail:
Inventory: INV Before:	After:

DATA BOX

Process:		# of Operators
Verb/Noun:		

Operator Cycle Time: OCT	
Machine Cycle Time: MCT	
Value-Added Time: VAT	
Changeover Time: C/O	
Quality: % Defects/Scrap Rate	
Productivity: Units/Person/Hour	
Total Space: Sq. Feet/Meters	
Value-Added Space: (sq.ft/m)	
Product Travel: Feet/Meters	
Product Flow: Push/Pull	Push Pull
Information Flow: Manual/Electronic	Manual Elec.
Shifts: NET Avail. Time (Sec.)	Net Avail:
Inventory: INV Before:	After:

DATA BOX

ENNA

Process:		# of Operators
Verb/Noun:		

Operator Cycle Time: OCT	
Machine Cycle Time: MCT	
Value-Added Time: VAT	
Changeover Time: C/O	
Quality: % Defects/Scrap Rate	
Productivity: Units/Person/Hour	
Total Space: Sq. Feet/Meters	
Value-Added Space: (sq.ft/m)	
Product Travel: Feet/Meters	
Product Flow: Push/Pull	Push Pull
Information Flow: Manual/Electronic	Manual Elec.
Shifts: NET Avail. Time (Sec.)	Net Avail:
Inventory: INV Before:	After:

DATA BOX

ENNA © Enna 2009
www.enna.com

Process:		# of Operators
Verb/Noun:		

Operator Cycle Time: OCT	
Machine Cycle Time: MCT	
Value-Added Time: VAT	
Changeover Time: C/O	
Quality: % Defects/Scrap Rate	
Productivity: Units/Person/Hour	
Total Space: Sq. Feet/Meters	
Value-Added Space: (sq.ft/m)	
Product Travel: Feet/Meters	
Product Flow: Push/Pull	Push Pull
Information Flow: Manual/Electronic	Manual Elec.
Shifts: NET Avail. Time (Sec.)	Net Avail:
Inventory: INV Before:	After:

DATA BOX

Process:		# of Operators
Verb/Noun:		

Operator Cycle Time: OCT	
Machine Cycle Time: MCT	
Value-Added Time: VAT	
Changeover Time: C/O	
Quality: % Defects/Scrap Rate	
Productivity: Units/Person/Hour	
Total Space: Sq. Feet/Meters	
Value-Added Space: (sq.ft/m)	
Product Travel: Feet/Meters	

Product Flow: Push/Pull	Push	Pull
Information Flow: Manual/Electronic	Manual	Elec.

Shifts: NET Avail. Time (Sec.)	Net Avail:

Inventory: INV	Before:	After:

DATA BOX

ENNA

Process:		# of Operators
Verb/Noun:		

Operator Cycle Time: OCT	
Machine Cycle Time: MCT	
Value-Added Time: VAT	
Changeover Time: C/O	
Quality: % Defects/Scrap Rate	
Productivity: Units/Person/Hour	
Total Space: Sq. Feet/Meters	
Value-Added Space: (sq.ft/m)	
Product Travel: Feet/Meters	
Product Flow: Push/Pull	Push Pull
Information Flow: Manual/Electronic	Manual Elec.
Shifts: NET Avail. Time (Sec.)	Net Avail:
Inventory: INV Before:	After:

DATA BOX

ENNA.

© Enna 2009
www.enna.com

Process:		# of Operators
Verb/Noun:		

Operator Cycle Time: OCT	
Machine Cycle Time: MCT	
Value-Added Time: VAT	
Changeover Time: C/O	
Quality: % Defects/Scrap Rate	
Productivity: Units/Person/Hour	
Total Space: Sq. Feet/Meters	
Value-Added Space: (sq.ft/m)	
Product Travel: Feet/Meters	
Product Flow: Push/Pull	Push Pull
Information Flow: Manual/Electronic	Manual Elec.
Shifts: NET Avail. Time (Sec.)	Net Avail:
Inventory: INV Before:	After:

DATA BOX

ENNA.

© Enna 2009
www.enna.com

Process:		# of Operators
Verb/Noun:		

Operator Cycle Time: OCT	
Machine Cycle Time: MCT	
Value-Added Time: VAT	
Changeover Time: C/O	
Quality: % Defects/Scrap Rate	
Productivity: Units/Person/Hour	
Total Space: Sq. Feet/Meters	
Value-Added Space: (sq.ft/m)	
Product Travel: Feet/Meters	
Product Flow: Push/Pull	Push Pull
Information Flow: Manual/Electronic	Manual Elec.
Shifts: NET Avail. Time (Sec.)	Net Avail:
Inventory: INV Before:	After: